Still Crazy
for Horses

Karen Briggs
and
Shawn Hamilton

Scholastic Canada Ltd.
New York Toronto London Auckland
Sydney Mexico City New Delhi Hong Kong

To Kibbles, for 16 years of fun and many more to come.
To my parents for my first pony, Tommy, and my first camera!!
A special thanks to my assistants, Nicky, Lesa and Dorothy.
— Shawn Hamilton

This one is for my parents, who put up with my own horse craziness . . .
and for Toddy, my intrepid equine companion.
— Karen Briggs

Scholastic Canada Ltd.
175 Hillmount Road, Markham, Ontario, Canada L6C 1Z7

Scholastic Inc.
555 Broadway, New York, NY 10012, USA

Scholastic Australia Pty Limited
PO Box 579, Gosford, NSW 2250, Australia

Scholastic New Zealand Limited
Private Bag 94407, Greenmount, Auckland, New Zealand

Scholastic Publications Ltd.
Villiers House, Clarendon Avenue, Leamington Spa, Warwickshire CV32 5PR, UK

National Library of Canada Cataloguing in Publication Data

Briggs, Karen, 1963-
Still crazy for horses

ISBN 0-439-98776-8

1. Horses — Juvenile literature. I. Hamilton, Shawn, 1961-
II. Title.

SF302.B762 2001   j636.1   C2001-930283-5

6 5 4 3 2 1   Printed in Canada   1 2 3 4 5/0

A Foal Is Born

It takes eleven long months for a foal to grow inside his mother. Mares usually give birth in the spring, and almost always at night. The reason for this is that horses are prey animals, and when they give birth in the wild the mare and foal are both vulnerable to predators that are attracted by the smell of blood. Hidden by darkness, the mare and foal have a better chance of survival. Domestic horses retain this age-old instinct even though it's very unlikely they will be preyed upon by a cougar or other attacker, so most mare owners expect to spend several sleepless nights in the barn when the foal is due.

Mares can be sneaky, too. Even though there are signs that they are about to foal, they might keep their owner waiting in vain for the big event, then give birth the moment they're left alone for a while. Since the birth can happen in less than an hour, it can be very easy to miss. Horses almost always have only one offspring at a time. Twins do occur, but they usually don't survive.

Once the foal is born, he will try to stand up almost immediately. The mare will nicker at her new youngster, and lick him dry with her tongue, then help nudge him to his feet with her nose. His first few attempts will be clumsy — his legs are very long and wobbly and it's difficult for him to control them! But after a few false starts, the newborn will usually find his balance, and take his first steps within an hour of his arrival. Once the foal is on his feet, the umbilical cord (which connects the mare to her baby) breaks. The stump is dipped in a little disinfectant solution to help prevent infection.

It's important that the new foal nurse from his mother within the first

few hours of his life. The milk his mother provides during this time is called colostrum — just like a human mother's. It is rich in antibodies which will help protect the new foal from diseases. Sometimes it takes a little while before the foal finds the mare's udder and figures out how to suckle, but he is born hungry, so he'll keep trying until he gets it. After he drinks his fill, he will curl up and go to sleep. Being born is a tiring business!

By morning the foal is usually much sturdier on his legs, and ready to keep up with his mother, even at a trot or canter. This, too, is essential for a prey animal — it must be able to keep up with the herd. In a couple of days, most foals are bucking and playing and running circles around their mothers. But they never stray too far, for if danger should threaten they prefer to hide behind mom's big, solid body.

As a foal grows, he gets more confident, and starts to explore his environment. He will also start to sample solid food by the time he is a couple of weeks old, following his mother's example and tasting what she eats. He will continue to nurse, though, several times an hour, until he is four to six months old.

By fall the foal and mare will be ready to go their separate ways. This process is called weaning, and while it is upsetting to them both for a day or two, it's a necessary part of growing up. In the spring the foal will be a yearling, and will look more like a gangly teenager than a kid. Though horses grow much faster than humans, it will still be another year or more before he will be mature enough to wear a saddle or harness. Most horses begin their training as two- or three-year-olds.

The official birthday of every Thoroughbred and Standardbred foal born in North America is January 1. In Australia and New Zealand, every foal has an official birthday of August 1. This simplifies things when races are scheduled, because all horses the same "age" race only against each other. But it also means that a foal born right after the official "birthday" will always have an advantage over a horse born months later, because it will be larger and more mature.

If you don't know your horse's birthday, you may be able to estimate his age by looking at his teeth. A horse's teeth grow throughout his lifetime, and they change shape as he gets older, too. It takes practice to be able to age a horse well by his teeth, and after the horse is about seven, it's harder to be accurate because the signs are more difficult to distinguish.

Facing page: Tennessee Walking Horse

Rocky Mountain Horse

When you're traveling in the rugged mountains and foothills of the Appalachian Mountains, far from civilization, you need a companion who really knows the lay of the land. If your partner is a sure-footed, gentle Rocky Mountain Horse, then you can be sure you're in good company and will make it safely home. (The "rocky" refers to the native terrain of this breed, not to the Rocky Mountains of the American West.)

Like his close cousin, the Tennessee Walking Horse, the Rocky Mountain Horse is a gaited horse. He walks and canters just like other horses, but instead of trotting he performs a special single-foot gait (with only a single foot off the ground at any one time) which is very comfortable for the rider. In fact, the single-foot movement makes him ideal for beginner riders and older folks. And because he always has at least three feet on the ground, he is steady and sure-footed even in rocky, steep terrain. The Rocky Mountain Horse is very popular for taking tourists up and down mountain trails in the eastern United States, and he is also a favorite with forest rangers and mounted police officers.

Almost all Rocky Mountain Horses descend from a single stallion named Old Tobe, who was owned by a Kentucky farmer named Sam Tuttle. Old Tobe was said to be as gentle as a kitten and as clever on the trails as a mountain goat. He sired fine foals right up to the ripe old age of 37.

Today's Rocky Mountain Horses are known for being unusually tough and hardy, just like their foundation sire. They need no special pampering or fancy feed to keep them healthy, and they have great endurance for long journeys. Their special ground-covering gait makes it easy for both horse and rider to cover vast distances before getting tired. Though some have started to make appearances in the show ring in recent years, it is as wonderful trail horses that the breed is most appreciated.

Fast Fact

Rocky Mountain Horses come in many colors, but one of the most beautiful and unique is silver dapple — a chocolate-brown body, often with dappled markings, paired with a silvery gray or flaxen mane and tail. Only a few other breeds in the world, including the Shetland pony, have this special coat color.

Friesian

The jet-black Friesian looks like something out of a fantasy or a romance novel — the kind of horse the hero should gallop in on to rescue someone in distress! With his proud bearing and luxuriant wavy mane and tail, he has been a star of the circus and the movie screen. But he was bred to be a fine carriage horse, a job at which he still excels.

The Friesian originated in Friesland, a province in the northern part of the Netherlands (Holland). The Dutch people who live there are great horse enthusiasts, and they have carefully guarded the Friesian bloodlines for hundreds of years. Friesian horses were famous throughout Europe for their beauty, strength and high-stepping movement, and were the favored mounts of kings and queens. They were sturdy enough to do light farm work too, but in harness they really made an impression. Imagine a team of four perfectly matched, gleaming black Friesians pulling your coach — that was the way to arrive in style.

Today the Dutch are still very strict about maintaining the special qualities of their horses. It's not enough for a Friesian foal to be born of two registered parents. He must also pass two inspections, one when he is a baby and another when he is three years old, before he can be accepted into the studbook as a Friesian. Only the very best individuals are kept for breeding, and cross-breeding with other types of horses is not allowed.

Friesians remain wonderful driving horses, and they are becoming more and more popular in North America for pulling carriages. But they are also impressive in the dressage ring, where they look almost as if they are dancing with their riders. Though they usually stand no taller than about 15:3 hands, their high head carriage gives them an air of nobility and makes them look much larger. Friesians also sport lots of "feathers," fine hair that grows on their lower legs and around their hoofs and helps to emphasize their high-stepping action. Trimming that hair, or shortening the mane or tail (which often sweeps the ground) is frowned upon. Friesians are always black. A small white star on the forehead is the only permissible marking.

Fast Fact

If you would like to ride or own a Friesian, you might have to do a bit of searching. There are only about 2000 of them in North America, and they are quite expensive. But you can see these noble horses in dressage and driving competitions — and of course on the movie screen! Friesians appeared in the films *Ladyhawke* and *Gladiator*.

Akhal-Teke

From the harsh desert land of Turkmenistan, near Russia, comes a horse so rare and fine that he seems to be made of gold. He's the Akhal-Teke, a breed so ancient that some say he pre-dates even the Arabian.

If you are lucky enough to see an Akhal-Teke, you'll notice right away how unusual he is. He's tall, lean and slender, like a greyhound, with a long neck and a sparse mane and tail. But the most striking thing about him is the beautiful golden glow of his coat. No matter what color he is — bay, black, dun, palomino or chestnut — he sparkles in the sun as if he were metallic.

The Akhal-Teke's name is a combination of Akhal, the name for an oasis in the foothills of the Kopet Dag Mountains (once a part of ancient Persia) and Teke, another name for the nomadic Turkmen tribe who treasured these horses for many centuries.

In a land where conditions were harsh and food was scarce, a good horse was essential to a tribesman's survival. They were a source of great pride, and treated as members of the family. To this day, Akhal-Tekes bond closely with their owners but are suspicious of strangers. They are said to be such good judges of character that in Turkmenistan, they were used to discover whether a woman's suitor was a sincere and good man. If the family's Akhal-Teke horse didn't like the man, the marriage was off!

Akhal-Tekes are true desert horses, with extraordinary powers of endurance. They are known for their ability to cover vast distances with little food or water. (In their homeland, they often survived by being fed balls of barley and mutton fat when there was no grazing.) Their swiftness, grace and sensitive natures have made them famous in Russia and Asia, but they are only starting to be discovered in North America. Fewer than a hundred Akhal-Tekes have been brought to Canada and the United States so far — but as more people discover this exotic and lovely horse, he will not be a secret for much longer!

Fast Fact

Some historians now think that the Akhal-Teke may have played a part in the development of the Thoroughbred, the fastest racehorse in the world. Three Arabian stallions are said to have founded the Thoroughbred breed in the late 1600s and early 1700s: the Godolphin Arabian, the Byerly Turk and the Darley Arabian. Research on the origins of the Byerly Turk now tells us that he may not have been an Arabian at all, but an Akhal-Teke, who probably contributed to the long, lean looks of the Thoroughbred.

Clydesdale

The pride of Scotland is the noble Clydesdale horse. Of all the draft breeds, it's the Clydesdale that is the flashiest, fanciest horse in harness. He sports big splashes of white on his face, on his legs (often reaching up past his knees and hocks), and sometimes even on his belly. And this gentle giant has lots of silky "feathers" on his legs, which sway like a decorative fringe as he trots down the road or across the show ring.

The Clydesdale breed takes its name from the River Clyde, which flows through the region of Scotland in which he first originated back in the mid-1700s.

Before the days of tractors and trucks, Clydesdales were used not only to help farmers plow their fields, but also to haul coal and other heavy items through the streets of Glasgow and Edinburgh, two of Scotland's major cities. Because they often worked on very hard, rough cobblestone streets, it was important that Clydesdales pick their feet up smartly so they would not trip. Even today Clydes are known for the way they snap up their hoofs with every step. They are also renowned for their natural strength and for their huge hoofs, each one the size of a dinner plate.

The Clydesdale is taller and has longer legs than many other draft breeds, such as the Belgian and the Percheron. He may stand 18 hands or taller and usually weighs between 700 and 1000 kilograms (1500 and 2000 pounds). Clyde stallions can weigh even more — up to 1100 kilograms (2400 pounds) — as much as a small car! Bay and roan (a solid body color but with white hairs sprinkled throughout the horse's coat) are a Clydesdale's most common colors, but he can also be brown, chestnut, black — even spotted. They almost always have a wide blaze or a "bald face," and white markings on their legs.

When Clydesdales are crossed with Thoroughbreds, they often pass on their white markings to their offspring. These Clydesdale-Thouroughbred crosses are very popular for fox-hunting and jumping.

Fast Fact

You have probably seen Clydesdales in TV advertisements, pulling a big red wagon or galloping through the snow. These thundering Clydes have become some of the most famous horses in the world!

Connemara

The Connemara pony is renowned for both its stamina and its jumping ability. The breed comes from the mountainous, barren terrain of Connemara in western Ireland. Ancient Celts are thought to have first brought ponies to the Emerald Isle over 2500 years ago to draw their war chariots, and in the 1700s some Arabian and Thoroughbred blood was introduced to the native stock to lend it more elegance. Today's Connemara ponies often show the dished facial profile that proves that Arabian influence.

Connemaras are hard and willing workers. Over the centuries Irish farmers depended on the sturdy ponies to toil from dawn till dusk, tilling the land, pulling a cart, dragging seaweed from the shores to fertilize the fields, carrying turf (peat moss) from the bogs to be burned as fuel on the hearth, and toting the family children to church on Sunday. As if this weren't enough, they were often used for fox-hunting and racing on the farmer's days of leisure. The ease with which Connemaras do all these things, even today, is a testament to their natural toughness.

The tallest of the nine kinds of British native ponies (ranging from 13 to 14:2 hands, with some individuals reaching horse size), the Connemara breed has produced some outstanding showjumpers and three-day eventers, who have competed on equal footing with horses far larger. A 15-hand Connemara called The Nugget became a *puissance* (high-jumping) champion, clearing a 2.18-meter (over 7-foot) barrier at the Olympia Horse Show in London, England, in 1935 — and he was 22 years old at the time! Stroller, the famous 14:1-hand showjumper who won a silver medal at the 1968 Olympic Games, was half Connemara. And more recently the little Connemara stallion Erin Go Bragh, piloted by Carol Koslowski, was one of the toughest competitors at the advanced level of three-day eventing in the United States during the 1990s.

Connemaras are most commonly dun or gray in color, but they can also be black, bay, chestnut, palomino or any other solid color. They are blessed with an excellent sloping shoulder, which gives them a long stride and a nimble jump, plus short, tough cannon bones, which help them avoid injury.

Connemaras are also celebrated for their sensible dispositions. Their popularity with both children and adults has extended worldwide. There are now Connemara Pony Societies established in at least 17 countries on 4 continents.

Fast Fact

The largest display of Connemara ponies in the world takes place every August at the Clifden Connemara Show in Ireland, a show that has been held every year since 1924. Over 400 ponies, from majestic breeding stallions to frisky foals, are brought from all over the Emerald Isle to take part.

Bashkir Curly

Have you ever seen a horse with curly eyelashes, curly hairs in his ears, and waves or ringlets all over his body? He's the Bashkir Curly, the horse who thinks he's a poodle!

No one is sure exactly where horses with crinkly coats came from. We do know that young Peter Damele and his father, who lived in the remote high country of central Nevada, spotted three of these unique horses running wild in the mountains when they went out riding one day back in 1898. They captured a chestnut-colored Curly horse and broke him to ride. He proved to be a versatile, sensible and sure-footed ranch horse. Soon the Damele family noticed that not only was the curly coat eye-catching, it was practical too. The Curly horses survived the harsh mountain winters better than other horses.

So the family began to breed the wavy-coated horses. They named the breed Bashkir Curly because they had heard about a Russian breed of horse called the Bashkir that was supposed to be curly too. That turned out to be a case of mistaken identity, but other curly-coated horses have turned up from time to time in history, in places as far apart as South America, Europe and India.

Today the Bashkir Curly is popular as a ranch and pleasure horse. He's not only tough and sure-footed, he's also intelligent and friendly. His coat comes in just about every color, including pinto and Appaloosa-spotted, and may be only slightly wavy (looking a little like crushed velvet) or curled in tight corkscrews all over the body. He usually looks curlier in the winter when his coat is longer. In the summer he may shed his mane hair, and sometimes his tail hair too, growing them back when the weather turns cold. He's a small and compact horse, usually standing between 14 and 15 hands high, with a body shape rather like the Morgan. But it's his luxuriant curls that people notice first!

Fast Fact

If you have an allergy to horsehair, then the Bashkir Curly may be the horse for you! His wavy coat is hypoallergenic, which means it won't make you sneeze the way normal horsehair will. Many people who are allergic to horses can ride and enjoy being around a Bashkir Curly.

Haflinger

If you lived in the steep mountainous country of the Tyrolean Alps in Austria and northern Italy, you might depend on a pair of skis for transportation in the winter. But in the summer the best way of getting from place to place would be with the help of a sure-footed, sturdy Haflinger pony.

The Haflinger, who gets his name from the Austrian town of Hafling, is made for mountain travel. He can negotiate narrow, winding paths carrying a rider or a heavy load in a pack, and he is also adept at pulling a cart, wherever the roadway is wide enough. He is built like a miniature draft horse — broad of chest, tough and strong — but pony-sized, and able to survive on the sparse plants growing among the rocks.

For centuries, the Haflinger pony was the only reliable means of transportation for the mountain peasants who lived in the Alps, and he often lived as part of the family. He developed a friendly, forgiving temperament, which is one of his most prized characteristics today.

But the Haflinger isn't just helpful — he's beautiful too! He has lovely palomino coloring, ranging from pale cream, to the shade of a copper penny, to almost chocolatey, always with a thick, luxurious white mane and tail. This flashy coat makes him instantly recognizable all over the world.

All of today's Haflingers trace back to a single stallion by the name of 249 Folie, who was one-quarter Arabian. Folie's descendents are separated into seven different families, all of whom have records in the Haflinger studbook begun in 1874.

Haflingers have surprising strength and athleticism for their size (between 13:2 and 14:3 hands), and are now popular around the world as light draft and harness ponies. They are also wonderful to ride, being small enough for children, but sturdy enough to carry an adult with ease. And like many breeds of ponies, they are very clever, retaining all the wit that helps them survive on the mountain slopes.

Fast Fact

Austria is very proud of its native Haflingers. At the National Stud Farm called *Fohlenhof Ebbs*, you can see over 180 Haflinger stallions, mares and foals running free, and demonstrating their skills in dressage, jumping and in harness in a daily parade.

Norwegian Fjord

Exmoor Pony

Imagine the landscape of England a few hundred thousand years ago. There were swamps and forests, vast plains and mountains — and there were also woolly mammoths, huge bears and saber-toothed tigers! Living among these fierce creatures was a nimble little pony who survived predators (including Stone Age man, who regarded him as a tasty lunch) by his wits and his fleetness of foot.

What did he look like? Scientists think he was a lot like the present-day Exmoor pony, who seems hardly changed by all the passing years.

According to fossil records, the Exmoor's primitive characteristics represent the closest living link to the ancient wild ponies that roamed Great Britain during the Stone Age. Since Exmoor is a remote area known for its bleak, windswept plains and miserably wet, cold winters, the native ponies have been molded by nature for survival. They have an unusual double-layered winter coat, which provides both insulation (like thermal underwear) and waterproofing (like a raincoat), and they are also equipped with a "snow-chute," a patch of short, coarse hairs at the top of the tail to channel rain and snow away from the body. A unique feature of the breed is the "toad eye," an unusually heavy upper brow which helps protect the pony's eyes from wind and driving rain.

Only half a century ago the Exmoor pony was on the verge of becoming extinct. During the difficult years of World War II the ponies were neglected, used to feed starving British families — sometimes even used by the army for target practice!

By 1945 there were only about 50 purebred Exmoors left, but some dedicated breeders saved them. There are still only about 1200 Exmoor ponies worldwide, but more and more people are discovering their charms all the time.

These tiny ponies often stand no more than 12:3 hands, and weigh about 318 kilograms (700 pounds). In color they are all virtually identical shades of brown or bay, with oatmeal-shaded muzzles, light rings around the eyes and beige bellies. Their coloring, which helps them blend in well against their natural background of heather, grasses and bracken, aids them even today, for a few hundred native Exmoors still roam wild on a portion of the swampy plains known as moors. Each fall they are gathered for inspection and branding. Only foals who have the coloring and conformation of the ancient ponies earn the four-pointed star brand of the Exmoor Pony Society.

Fast Fact

Though wild and woolly Exmoor ponies are tiny, they are incredibly strong and can easily carry large adult riders weighing 77 kilograms (170 pounds) or more.

Hackney

People who want to attract attention today might drive a flashy sports car. But in the 1800s the best way to catch everyone's eye was to drive a high-stepping Hackney.

The Hackney horse and his miniature cousin, the Hackney pony, come from England, where they were bred to be the ultimate in elegance for pulling a carriage. As cities grew larger and as smooth, well-maintained roads started to replace rough and rutted carriage paths, the sturdy-but-slow cart horse fell out of favor. People wanted a lighter, faster horse to get them to their destinations on time and in style. The proud-looking Hackney, who took his name from the "hackney carts" which were available to be rented out (like the taxis of today), was just the ticket. He became instantly popular with the upper classes, who enjoyed hitching up their finest teams to gleaming carriages and driving through the streets and parks of London, just to be seen. The higher the Hackney snapped his knees and hocks, and the more fiery he looked, the more he impressed everyone.

Several different breeds contributed their unique qualities to the Hackney. From the Thoroughbred and the Arabian came beauty, refinement and stamina; from the Friesian and the Norfolk Trotter (a now-extinct breed), snappy action at the trot. In the 1880s a man named Christopher Wilson was responsible for developing the Hackney pony by breeding only small pony mares to his 14-hand Hackney stallion, Sir George. Today Hackney ponies outnumber Hackney horses, worldwide, by 20 to 1.

The Hackney horse and pony are still popular in the show ring, where they are harness specialists. In temperament they can be quite "hot" and excitable, but this only contributes to the dashing impression they make on the judge. Most Hackneys are bay in color, making it easy to find matching horses or ponies for a team, but they may also be chestnut, black or even spotted. Their naturally high head carriage, beautifully sculpted faces and piston-like action at the trot make them the true aristocrats of the show ring.

Fast Fact

Some Hackneys are shown with their tails docked (cut) to a very short length. This was the style for a fancy carriage horse in the 1800s. Fortunately the practice of docking tails is now falling out of favor, since it deprives the animal of his natural protection against flies.

Mustang

Few sights are as stirring as a herd of mustangs, running wild and free across the plains and through the canyons of the American West. You might think that mustangs have always roamed the remote mountain ranges of the West, but that's not really the case. Though fossil records show us that modern horses originated in North America, they mysteriously disappeared from the landscape about 10,000 years ago. It was only in the 1500s, when the Spanish invaded North America, that horses were re-introduced to this continent.

Over the years, as the Spanish continued to explore North America, they imported more and more of their Andalusian horses. The Native Americans quickly got over their fear of these unfamiliar creatures and began to see how useful they were, so they tried to build up the size of their own herds. Some of these horses escaped to run wild across the plains. Eventually they became known as mustangs, from the Spanish word *mestaño*, meaning stray or ownerless horse.

Today the mustang carries the blood of many different breeds in his veins. Cow ponies, draft horses, Thoroughbreds and Arabians also escaped from settlers heading west, or were turned loose to fend for themselves. These joined up with the herds of Spanish horses. As a result, the modern mustang comes in all shapes, sizes and colors. But two qualities are common — hardiness and intelligence. Only the strongest and most wily horses can survive a prairie winter with scarce food and no shelter.

Once there were over two million mustangs roaming the ranges of the North American West. But ranchers who settled these lands wanted to fence in the grassland for cattle. They considered mustangs competition for grazing land, and began to round them up and shoot them. By 1970 fewer than 17,000 wild horses remained, and people began to fear they might disappear forever. But the governments of the United States and Canada took action in the 1970s to protect these herds by designating certain lands for the mustang to roam undisturbed. The land available is limited, so every year some mustangs are rounded up and made available for adoption by hopeful horse owners.

Taming a mustang requires patience and experience, but it can be very rewarding. Because of their natural toughness and knowledge of the land, many mustangs become top ranch horses.

Fast Fact

In Lexington, Kentucky, there are 24 mustangs who were removed from the ranges in Wyoming when they were very young. Inner-city kids, many of whom have never before touched a horse, care for the mustangs and learn to ride them. They form the Kentucky Horse Park's Mustang Troop Drill Team, which has performed at major events and parades across the United States.

Newfoundland Pony

Early settlers to the forbidding, rocky island of Newfoundland on Canada's east coast brought with them sturdy ponies to help them tame the landscape. Historians know that Exmoor, Dartmoor, Welsh Mountain, Fell, Highland and Connemara ponies have all had a presence on the island over the centuries. Their bloodlines became intermingled to eventually produce the hardy Newfoundland pony of today, one well-suited to his harsh environment. He's not remarkably big, nor small, not a fancy stepper or a flashy show mount — but he can work hard all day, survive on the scarcest of pasture and never complain.

An integral part of the island way of life right up until the 1950s, Newfoundland ponies skidded timbers, hauled firewood, carried kelp to help fertilize the farmland and moved rocks for the farmers and fishermen. When they weren't needed they were turned loose to fend for themselves.

Times have always been hard in Newfoundland. The soil is poor and it is difficult to make a living from farming.

Also, as stocks of fish around the island dwindled, the people who drew their livelihood from the ocean became worried about their futures. In desperation many pony owners, barely surviving on what they scraped from the land and the sea, sold their ponies for dog food. By 1997 there were only 144 known Newfoundland ponies in all the world, and many of those were geldings and aged mares, not suitable for breeding.

Finally the government of Newfoundland took action, declaring the Newfoundland pony a Heritage Animal and making laws for registering and protecting them. Since then the population of Newfoundland ponies has been making a comeback, with the help of some dedicated breeders, both in Newfoundland and elsewhere in North America. Newfoundland ponies may be anywhere between 11 and 14:2 hands, and any color including spotted, though dark bays are most common. A steady, willing temperament, and an ability to grow plump on the most meager feed, are characteristics of all Newfoundlands.

Fast Fact

In 2000, Newfoundland pony enthusiast Mary Liebau embarked on a five-month solo trip across the island of Newfoundland, riding her two Newfoundland ponies and accompanied by her dog. The goal of the trip was to raise money and awareness for the hardy Newfoundland breed.

Australian Stock Horse

When the first European settlers arrived on the remote shores of Australia in 1788, they brought with them horses to help them tame the land. Some were Thoroughbreds from England, some were Spanish Andalusians, and some were desert Arabians and hardy Welsh and Indonesian ponies. Not all survived the long, difficult ocean voyage, but those that did had tough constitutions — just what was needed for the wild country of the land Down Under.

Over time the bloodlines of all these different types of horses and ponies mixed to create a uniquely Australian saddle horse, sturdy and strong. The settlers, bush rangers and stockmen (or farmers) all depended on him to carry them vast distances over rugged country. He was dubbed the Waler, after the colony of New South Wales, but later came to be known as the Australian Stock Horse.

It was as a cavalry horse that the Australian Stock Horse made a name for himself in the 1800s. The British army shipped some of these hardy horses to India in 1857, and soon found they were tougher and sounder than the local animals. The army began to prefer Australian horses to all others for their cavalry divisions. Walers were a favored mount for the armies that fought in the bloody Boer War in South Africa around 1900. Over 160,000 gave their lives in battle during World War I.

Fortunately, the days of waging war on horseback are now over, and the Australian Stock Horse has returned to doing what he does best — being an all-around ranch and riding horse. On the remote sheep stations of the Outback, the Australian Stock Horse is considered the best form of transportation for inspecting the flocks that roam over many thousands of acres. His intelligence and speed also make him popular for playing polo and polocrosse (a sport which is a combination of polo and lacrosse). And he is often used for campdrafting, a uniquely Australian sport in which a horse and rider separate a cow from the herd and then persuade it to follow a pattern in an arena.

Fast Fact

Australian Stock Horses took the spotlight at the opening ceremonies for the 2000 Sydney Olympics. An amazing group of 120 Australian Stock Horses, with riders ranging from ages 15 to 77, opened the Games by galloping into the main stadium and forming the five interlocking Olympic rings and other patterns, to the theme music from the movie, *The Man From Snowy River*. The performance was the largest musical ride ever assembled.

Percheron and Belgian

The powerful Percheron may look at home pulling a plow or a wagon, but the proud way he carries himself reveals his heritage as a charger who once carried armored knights into battle in medieval times. His ancestors fought in the Crusades, fierce religious wars that lasted for hundreds of years. Once the wars were finally over, this huge draft breed, weighing in at 700 kilograms (1600 pounds) or more, was pressed into service on the farm, where his great strength helped with many everyday tasks.

The modern Percheron gets his name from the French region of Le Perche , where he originates, but by the 1700s he could be found all over Europe. In 1839 the first Percheron was brought to the United States by ship, and soon the breed became a favorite of North American farmers. By 1930 there were three times as many registered Percherons in the U.S.A. as all other draft breeds combined.

Though they have now been replaced by tractors on the farm, Percherons remain popular in the show ring, where they can be seen in large teams of four, six or even eight horses pulling replicas of the heavy farm wagons of yesteryear. Percherons make good riding horses and are surprisingly graceful jumpers. They are almost always black or gray, but an occasional chestnut, bay or roan does occur. They stand between 16 and 18 hands, are heavily muscled, and have easygoing, steady temperaments, which make them a pleasure to work with.

Similar in build, but often even taller, is the big blond Belgian, a breed whose history began in the fertile farm country of Belgium in western Europe. Weighing up to a tonne (2400 pounds) and standing up to 18 hands high, he is a true draft horse, built for pulling heavy loads. But don't be fooled by his size, for beneath his chestnut coat and thick cream-colored mane is the soul of a very gentle giant.

Some Belgians still work the fields in Europe and North America. They are popular with Mennonite and Amish communities who prefer to farm with natural horsepower rather than mechanical means. They are also used to pull logs out of heavily wooded areas where tractors and trucks can't go. You're most likely to see Belgians at horse shows, exhibitions and parades. Because they are all the same color, it's easy to put together a matching hitch, all working together to pull their gleaming wagons. When a team of four or more Belgians thunders past you, you'll feel the ground shake!

Fast Fact

The Percheron is sometimes crossed with the Andalusian, a fiery Spanish horse, to produce a breed called the Spanish-Norman — a recreation of the war horse of medieval Europe. These are often used in jousting displays, featuring armored knights running at each other with their long poles called lances.

Trakehner

The athletic Trakehner (tra-KAY-ner) is a true survivor. He was bred as a horse of war . . . and it was because of war that the breed was nearly lost forever.

In the early 1700s King Friedrich Wilhelm I of Prussia (now part of Germany) wanted a lighter, faster cavalry horse for his troops. He established a royal stud farm at Trakehnen, and bred Arabian and Thoroughbred stallions with heavier German mares to create an elegant horse who covered the ground with long strides.

This new breed had such intelligence, willingness to work and versatility that it soon became the favorite of the king's army. Trakehners also excelled at sports such as showjumping, endurance riding and dressage. Only the finest horses were used to continue the bloodlines, and most of the breeding horses were housed at the royal stud right up to the 20th century.

But when the Second World War broke out, the future of the Trakehner was in danger, because the royal stud farm was right in the middle of the fighting. In the bitter winter of 1945, as it became clear that Germany was losing the war, huge armies started advancing from Russia. The home of the Trakehner horses was directly in their path. With most of the men already fighting, it was left to the women and children to save their beloved horses. They hitched the Trakehners to wagons loaded with their few belongings, and fled west. It would become a grueling 1000-kilometer (600-mile) journey, with the Russian army in close pursuit. The people and horses were shot at from the ground and from airplanes. Only about 100 of the original 800 horses made it to safety, and many of those suffered wounds and starvation.

After the war the German government began to take steps to re-establish the stud farm. Today Trakehners are bred not only in Germany but around the globe. They are prized by some of the world's top riders as showjumpers, dressage horses and three-day eventers, and have competed at many Olympics and international competitions.

Trakehners stand between 15:2 and 17:2 hands, come in most solid colors, and are best known for their beautiful, elastic way of moving, with a trot and canter which almost seem to float above the ground.

Fast Fact

One of the most famous Trakehners was a big gray Canadian-bred stallion named Abdullah. Ridden by Conrad Homfeld, he represented the United States at the 1984 Olympic Games in Los Angeles and won a Team Gold and an Individual Silver medal in showjumping. Later he became a famous sire of showjumpers. More recently, the Trakehner mare Larissa, ridden by Bruce Mandeville, represented Canada in the sport of three-day eventing at the 2000 Olympic Games in Australia.

Tennessee Walking Horse

If you love to ride, but don't like to be bounced around, then you'll fall in love with the glide ride of a Tennessee Walking Horse. When a Tennessee Walker performs his special gait, the running walk, his rider can sit almost motionless and watch the scenery go by. In fact, fans of this all-American breed boast that they can sip a cup of coffee while they ride and never spill a drop.

The Tennessee Walking Horse was originally developed by wealthy plantation owners in the state of Tennessee, much the way the American Saddlebred was developed in the southern United States. These men wanted a large and impressive horse on which they could tour their huge properties, and because many of them weren't expert riders, they needed a horse who was comfortable to ride. Many breeds contributed their special qualities to the Tennessee Walker, including the Morgan, the Standardbred, the Canadian, the Thoroughbred and the now-extinct Narrangasett Pacer. No one is sure which breed contributed the running walk, but all Tennessee Walkers are born knowing how to do it. They can keep going for hours without becoming tired, traveling at speeds of 10 to 20 kilometers (6 to 12 miles) per hour, and bobbing their heads in time to the four-beat rhythm. Even their ears flop back and forth with every gliding stride.

The Tennessee Walking Horse was so comfortable to ride that he soon became a favorite of country doctors and traveling preachers, who had to make long journeys on horseback. Today pleasure riders appreciate his smooth gaits and his sensible, laid-back temperament. Many people who can't ride a trotting horse because they have an injury or are physically challenged find they can ride a Tennessee Walker without pain. Tennessee Walkers are flashy, too — they come in many colors, including spotted, and they have long, luxurious manes and tails.

The Tennessee Walking Horse is ruggedly handsome, standing between 14:3 and 17 hands and weighing up to 500 kilograms (1100 pounds). He has a reputation for having very few problems with lameness, and often lives well into his thirties. Though he remains most popular in the southern United States, riders in other parts of the world are now discovering his wonderful glide ride too.

Fast Fact

Although most Tennessee Walkers are ridden for pleasure, a few are strictly show horses. These horses wear large, heavy pads on their feet, which encourage them to snap their knees higher and take exaggerated, ground-covering strides. Trainers call this movement the big lick, and it is much sought after. In fact, sometimes trainers have used cruel methods to encourage their show horses to perform the big lick, but fortunately there are now regulations forbidding this.

See page 3 for the full-page photo of the Tennessee Walking Horse.

Norwegian Fjord

A fjord (pronounced FEE-ord), a narrow channel or harbor that is surrounded by high cliffs, is common in Norway and throughout Scandinavia, where the Norwegian Fjord horse originated. This Fjord bears a striking resemblance to the horses painted on cave walls by Ice Age artists over 30,000 years ago. Considered one of the oldest and purest breeds in the world, the Fjord has been domesticated for over 4000 years, and was favored by the Vikings as a small-but-mighty war mount. He still thrives in the chilly Scandinavian country of Norway, but he's also popular in many other parts of the world . . . even if there's not much call for war mounts these days!

Present-day Norwegian Fjords retain many of the characteristics of primitive Asian wild horses, from whom they are thought to have descended. They have a distinctive dun coat (ranging from pale cream to dark honey-colored), a dark stripe down their spines called a dorsal stripe, and zebra-stripe markings on their legs. Many also sport a dark cross over their withers, similar to that seen on donkeys. The Norwegian Fjord's mane is also unique: the center hairs are dark, and the outer hair on either side is white. Fjord enthusiasts cut the mane short, in a traditional crescent shape, so it will stand upright. Then they trim the outer hairs slightly shorter than the inner dark hairs, so that the dramatic dark stripe is displayed.

Fjords stand about 13 to 15 hands and are broad and muscular in build, weighing an average of 400 to 550 kilograms (900 to 1200 pounds). Their heads, however, are refined and often slightly dished in profile, suggesting the influence of some long-ago Arabian blood. Fjords are known for their gentle, people-oriented personalities and their seemingly endless appetite for work. In Norway and throughout Scandinavia, they are popular for both riding and driving, and often serve as all-round family horses. They are also used for farm work in the steep hills and mountains.

Fast Fact

In his native Norway, the Fjord is known as the *Norges Fjordhest*. *Hest* is the Norwegian word for horse. Norwegian Fjord foals are born with very light, almost silvery coats. As they mature, their color darkens to dun.

See center spread for the poster of the Norwegian Fjord.

Riding School Horses

If you love horses and would like to get to know them better, one of the best ways is to take some riding lessons. At a lesson stable, you'll meet many different kinds of horses and ponies, from tiny to enormous, to suit all shapes and sizes of riders. Don't be too disappointed if they aren't the untamed horses of your fantasies, though! There probably won't be any fiery gray Arabian stallions or towering black Friesians for you to ride at a lesson stable. Such horses are usually only suitable for professional riders with many years of experience.

Instead, the horses and ponies used for riding lessons — usually called school horses — are chosen for their patience, their wisdom and their gentleness with kids. They may not be majestic, or even purebred; in fact, they're far more likely to be a mixture of different breeds (called a cross-bred or a grade horse). Their looks may be a far cry from the pictures of the sleek and beautiful horses on your bedroom wall. They aren't glamorous show horses with fluttering ribbons in their manes or the ability to soar over Olympic-sized fences, and they won't win any races against fleet-footed Thoroughbreds. But what they lack in flashiness and speed, they make up for by being remarkable teachers.

It takes a very special horse or pony to teach a beginner to ride. Not every horse has the patience to put up with all the unintentional mistakes a new rider will make as he or she is learning. Many school horses are in their teens, or twenties — or even thirties — and have taught hundreds of people in their careers. Riding instructors know that a good school horse is worth his weight in gold, even if he doesn't have a fancy pedigree.

Wild and Free

Horses and ponies living wild are officially called feral — that is, they are the descendants of horses that once were domesticated by humans, and either escaped or were set free to fend for themselves. But even if their great-great-great-grandparents served humans under saddle or in harness, feral horses behave just like truly wild ones. They form small herds or bands, consisting of a number of mares, some foals and yearlings, and a single stallion who protects the group from predators and rival stallions. They are naturally shy and suspicious of humans, and when danger threatens, their first instinct is to gallop away rather than fight. They survive on the plants they can find in their environment, and often travel great distances to seek water or better grazing. They usually live in very remote and forbidding places, and endure harsh weather and other hardships. Only the strongest and the smartest survive.

Some feral horses scrape out a living on remote islands. One of the most famous is the Chincoteague pony, a breed that lives on the narrow sandbar islands of Chincoteague (pronounced SHIN-ko-teeg) and Assateague, off the coast of Maryland and Virginia in the northeastern United States.

Legend has it that the Chincoteague ponies first came to the islands when a 16th-century Spanish galleon was shipwrecked, but it is more likely that they are the descendants of animals turned out on the islands by 17th-century mainland farmers so that they wouldn't have to pay taxes for owning horses! Chincoteague and Assateague are harsh places to live — storms, even hurricanes, are always a threat, and the natural vegetation is tough and hard to chew. To find fresh water, the horses must paw holes in the sand. These conditions have stunted the horses to pony size (about 12 to 13 hands, on average) and made them very tough and wily.

Other pony populations live on tiny islands scattered along North America's east coast. They include the Banker ponies of Shackleford Island and the Outer Banks of North Carolina, and the tiny Sable Island ponies, who inhabit a sandbar far out in the Atlantic, 200 kilometres (120 miles) east of Canada's Nova Scotia coast. These ponies share similar traits — small size, toughness and thick, unruly manes and tails that help protect them from the elements. They are very suspicious of humans, but when captured and patiently tamed, can sometimes become great companions for children.

For more information:

AHKAL-TEKE
Akhal Teke Association of America
P.O. Box 114
Livermore, Colorado 80536 USA
http://members.tripod.com/
akhaltekeamerica/ATAA.html

AUSTRALIAN STOCK HORSE
The Australian Stock Horse Society Ltd.
P.O. Box 288
92 Kelly Street
Scone, New South Wales 2337
Australia
http://www.ashs.com/au

BASHKIR CURLY
Canadian Curly Horse Association
R.R. #1
Bowden, Alberta , Canada T0M 0K0
http://www.telusplanet.net/public/bnchorse/

American Bashkir Curly Horse Registry
P.O. Box 246
Ely, Nevada 89301-0246 USA
http://www.abcregistry.org

BELGIAN
Canadian Belgian Horse Association
17150 Concession 10
R.R. #3
Schomberg, Ontario, Canada L0G 1T0
http://www.canadianbelgianhorse.com/

Belgian Draft Horse Corporation
    of America
P.O. Box 335
Wabash, Indiana 46992-0335 USA
http://www.belgiancorp.com

CLYDESDALE
Clydesdale Horse Association of Canada
R.R. #2
Thornton, Ontario, Canada L0L 2N0
http://clrc.on.ca/clydesda.html

Clydesdale Breeders of the USA
17378 Kelley Road
Pecatonica, Illinois 61063 USA
http://www.clydesusa.com

CONNEMARA
American Connemara Pony Society
2360 Hunting Ridge Road
Winchester, VA 22603 USA
http://www.acps.org

EXMOOR
Canadian Mountain and Moorland Society
P.O. Box 155
Ripley, Ontario, Canada N0G 2R0

American Exmoor Pony Registry
c/o American Livestock Breeds Conservancy
Box 477
Pittsboro, North Carolina 27312-0477 USA

FRIESIAN
Friesian Horse Association of
    North America
P.O. Box 11217
Lexington, Kentucky
40574-1217 USA
http://www.fhana.com

**HACKNEY HORSE
AND PONY**
Canadian Hackney Society
7737 Dalmony Road
Osgoode, Ontario, Canada K0A 2W0
http://www.clrc.on.ca/hackney.html

American Hackney Horse Society
4059 Iron Works Pike, Suite #3
Lexington, Kentucky
40511-8462 USA
http://www.hackneysociety.com

HAFLINGER
Canadian Haflinger Association,
c/o Jan Hayward, Secretary/Treasurer
R.R.# 1
Grand Bend, Ontario, Canada N0M 1T0
http://www.haflinger.ca

Haflinger Breeders Organization, Inc.
14640 State Route 83
Coshocton, Ohio 43812-8911 USA
http://stallionstation.com/hbo

MUSTANG
North American Mustang Association
    and Registry
P.O. Box 850906
Mesquite, Texas
75185-0906 USA

Spanish Mustang National Registry
11790 Halstad Avenue South
Lonsdale, Minnesota 55046 USA
http://www.spanishmustang.org

NEWFOUNDLAND PONY
Newfoundland Pony Society
Box 5022
St. John's, Newfoundland.,
Canada A1C 5V3
http://www.gov.nf.ca/agric/
Click on "Heritage Animals"

NORWEGIAN FJORD
Canadian Fjord Horse Association
P.O. Box 1335
Killarney, Manitoba, Canada R0K 1G0
http://www.cfha.org/cfha

Norwegian Fjord Horse Registry
P.O. Box 685
Webster, New York
14580-9129 USA
http://www.nfhr.com

PERCHERON
Canadian Percheron Association
Kathy Ackles, Secretary/Treasurer
Box 1504
Vernon, British Columbia
Canada V1T 8C2
http://junction.net/~percheron

Percheron Horse Association of America
P.O. Box 141
10330 Quaker Road
Fredericktown, Ohio 43019 USA
http://www.percheronhorse.org

ROCKY MOUNTAIN HORSE
International Rocky Mountain Horse
    Association
P.O. Box 286
Paris, Kentucky 40362-0286 USA
http://www.rmhorse.com

**TENNESSEE
WALKING HORSE**
Canadian Registry of the Tennessee
    Walking Horse
P.O. Box 246
Postal Station M
Calgary, Alberta, Canada T2P 2H9
http://www.crtwh.ca

Tennessee Walking Horse Breeder's
    and Exhibitor's Association
P.O. Box 286
Lewisburg, Tennessee 37091 USA
http://www.twhbea.com

TRAKEHNER
Canadian Trakehner Horse Society
P.O. Box 1270
New Hamburg, Ontario,
Canada N0B 2G0
http://www.cantrak.on.ca

American Trakehner Association
1520 West Church Street
Newark, Ohio 43055 USA
http://www.americantrakehner.com

NOTE: addresses and website information are
accurate at the time of publication.